FRANK ORMSBY

# A Store of Candles

OXFORD LONDON NEW YORK
OXFORD UNIVERSITY PRESS
1977

Oxford University Press, Walton Street, Oxford OX2 6DP

OXFORD LONDON GLASGOW NEW YORK
TORONTO MELBOURNE WELLINGTON CAPE TOWN
IBADAN NAIROBI DAR ES SALAAM LUSAKA
KUALA LUMPUR SINGAPORE JAKARTA HONG KONG
TOKYO DELHI BOMBAY CALCUTTA MADRAS KARACHI

**British Library Cataloguing in Publication Data**

Ormsby, Frank

A store of candles.
I. Title
821'.9'14    PR6065.R/    77–30102
ISBN 0-19-211870-6

*Printed in Great Britain by
The Bowering Press Ltd. Plymouth*

*For Molly, Paula and Sean*

# ACKNOWLEDGEMENTS

Acknowledgements are due to the editors of the following magazines and anthologies in which some of these poems have appeared: *Austin Clarke Memorial Broadsheet, Capella, Caret, Choice* (Goldsmith Press), *Community Forum, Encounter, Era, Focus, Gown, Hibernia, The Honest Ulsterman, Irish Poets 1924–74, Irish Times, Lines Review, New Irish Writing* (Irish Press), *The New Review, The Niagara Magazine, Outposts, P.E.N. New Poems 1975–76* (Hutchinson), *Poetry Dimension 4* (Robson Books), *Poetry Nation, Poets from Ulster, Pyramid, Soundings* (Blackstaff Press), *Ten Irish Poets* (Carcanet Press), *U.C.D. Broadsheet, The Wearing of the Black* (Blackstaff Press). Some have appeared in the pamphlet collections *Ripe for Company* and *Business As Usual,* both from Ulsterman Publications. Some were broadcast on B.B.C. Radio 3 and Radio 4. 'Floods' was commissioned by the Arts Council of Northern Ireland for its series of poster/poems; the artist was John Middleton.

# CONTENTS

# THE PRACTICAL FARMS

1 *The Small Ads*
The small ads give notice of a world
Where little is wasted. All that is practical
Is in demand and someone will sell,
Linkbox and harrow, milk-churn and steel can
And paling post in search of new masters.
For heavy working boots Balfour's Your Man.


These packed columns counteract the news
Of drunken quarrels, troublesome buffoons
In country courtrooms. The dead hours in pubs,
At gable ends, diminish. Men who live
By sweat and commerce share the pointed ways
Of sober print—terse, almost oppressive.


2 *Economies*
In the plot next to the dairy whitewashed
Stones define a garden. A balding tyre
Renews itself as a circular
Flowerbed and panelling the greenhouse
Tacked polythene bags magnify sunlight.

The patron of new leases seems to smile
On all such couplings—lids as drinking-troughs,
Beans in biscuit tins on the henhouse roof.
Harmless for now the ladder's makeshift rung,
Weedkiller in lemonade bottles.


3 *A Fly in the Water*
The cool of the evening,
the whole lough belongs
to a man in a rowboat.
From here it seems his sole aim
is to reach the centre,
so straight his prow,
so bare the far shore
of coves and beaches.
I'd like to think he has cast off
by choice from the practical farms,
his leisurely track
a clean act of indulgence.
Closer, though, I trace
a line's trail in the water,
just in case.

# LANDSCAPE WITH FIGURES

What haunts me is a farmhouse among trees
Seen from a bus window, a girl
With a suitcase climbing a long hill
And a woman waiting.
The time the bus took to reach and pass
The lane's entrance nothing was settled,
The girl still climbing and the woman still
On the long hill's summit.

Men were not present. Neither in the fields
That sloped from hedges, nor beyond the wall
That marked the yard's limits
Was there sign of hens, or hands working.
No sight that might have softened
On the eye the scene's
Relentlessness.

Nothing had happened, yet the minute spoke
And the scene spoke and the silence,
And oppressed as air does, loading
For a storm's release.

All lanes and houses
Secretive in trees and gaunt hills' jawlines
Turn my thoughts again
To that day's journey and the thing I saw
And could not fathom. Struck with the same dread
I seem to share in sense, not detail,
What was heavy there:
Sadness of dim places, obscure lives,
Ends and beginnings,
Such extremities.

# WET LEAVES

The poignancy of wet leaves that drip
On the roadside. They bead and bead
And cushion to be shed in secret.
They hold until their tears' weight will hold
No longer, drop into the air those forms
That know but short perfection. In grass
They lose themselves and under the stones.


Caught the first time after a shower
That glint in leaves, it seemed the soft release
Of pent-up countrysides. Those muffled falls
Among the laurel beds belied the land's
Hardness. Never again would dour fields lie
Quite so forbidding, stones be so bare,
The dry eyes of countrymen never so cold.

# CAVES

The maps record only the townlands,
The daylight world that even strangers know
As field and farm. It rains on the hills,
The hillsides drink it in. The country steams
And watches clouds passing.


But here there is a darker underland.
Moon milk and cave coral sprout below
In sinks and shakeholes. Quietly they fill.
In Fathers' Hole and Cradle Pot the streams
Are massing.

# A NEW NEIGHBOUR

His is the house that always looks away,
Its back kitchen jutting on the lane
With curtains drawn. That cold gable angled
To the hedge, the gate's black barring
And the childless yard, are what we place him by.

By day he walks the boundaries with a gun,
As once he did before his heart tired
Of dark shapes crossing a border farm
And cratered roads. Meeting him we are not surprised
Not to be greeted and are silent too.

Tonight his lamp might be a flake of light
Peeled from a window. Daylight memories
Place it—by a shed, a whitewashed dairy—
But darkness hides what purpose takes him there,
And three fields' distance whether he sings or sighs.

# OLD MAN ON A COUNTRY BUS

Peers for a stop still fifteen miles away,
Will not commit his parcel to a rack
So far above him, and cannot shake free
Of fears that after all his pesterings
Of peaked officials, depot office-girls,
He has caught the wrong bus.

Relief's a spring,
A pint of blood, rejuvenation pill,
That carries him along the aisle and down
The broad steps, bulked sideways. Evening will find
Him, pleased survivor, slippered by the wall,
Watching horizons over the half-door.

# MCQUADE

When McQuade went up for a ball
He came down with snow on his heels,
And when McQuade took a shot the goalie
Had to hitch-hike back to the field:
A legend from the tall decades behind,
Like 'Bawler' Donnelly and the Night of the Big Wind.

A quiet cancer stopped him, its tackle sly,
Decisive. Shocked, I watched him fall,
Saw Death collect him, easily as a loose ball.

# A DEATH IN THE MANSION

There was fitness in the way they waked him,
In the quiet gloom in the room where he died.
Grief was a private rhythm, a proper ritual
Of old sad sisters, weeping by candlelight.
The black aunts mourned for the one who had died in his
   sleep.


At least we imagined it so, cocked morbid as crows
In the orchard branches. The gables loomed
Dour as expected, the gaunt, knockered,
Presbyterian doors. The living tombed
In that house, the genteel dead, would wear black forever,


And, met on roads, the aunts with veiled faces
Would hold that hour's silence, the sisters share
Odours of wax, the secrecy of lace,
And death, death would be the smell of crab apples,
Moss in trees; green as the nettle leaves


We skirted, jumped like hares, on the way home.

# NATURAL HISTORY SECTION

Here the dead butterflies surmount their names,
The bright wings in poses that persuade
They never were clumsy. Rest in formation
Beauties that we knew alurch in a garden,
Were partial to as colour on the wing
And not to be numbered. Fixed in their sad
Squadrons they diminish, English Orange Tip,
Irish Common Blue.

And sadder than stuffed birds this cheep and trill,
Recorded birdsong. The glass eyes in the cases
Less unreal. From rook to curlew,
Plover to taped wren, it runs its gamut.
You think at last of *one* bird, caged
In the ceiling, in search of his own voice.
Amplified in all the tongues of his kind
He cries: 'Testing, testing.'

Drawn to a window we observe the world
That cannot be labelled. Here the exhibits,
Flickering at the eye, mock information.
That tick in the oak tree's chest might be a bird,
A leaf in its dancing. Contexts are endless,
Nothing seems alone or wholly identified:
Weeds drinking with flowers, moss on walls,
The raw panic under a wet stone.

# THE LEAF

There is nothing new to be said of leaves
In their autumn colours. Brushing a dry
Rustle from our feet on mellow pavements
They ask no more than to be swept aside.
Why should we notice them? The many ways
They shuffle and re-shuffle as we pass
Whisper too much their sameness to be heard.
No fresh shapes form to make us pause.

A silent entrance from the world of trees
This year, a dull leaf that found an open
Door, clung to the carpet, forces me to bend.
Before I close my fingers it has bared
Enough of veins and curled brittle corners
To claim remembrance. Now leaves have begun
Quietly to insist their singleness.
One leaf in the hall renews a season.

# CALENDARS

Miss Brown's had flowers, generous bouquets
Too lush to be true. Magees' favoured cats
On thick, warm rugs near glowing firebars,
Cats better off than we were. Others bore
Like bloated postcards all the brittle gloss
Of beauty spots killed by the camera.

Reihills' was the calendar I liked best.
Each year, above the perforated days
In sturdy profile, centred in the spell
Of fence and paddock, stood the proof we craved
That one outsider made it by a head

Or that last year not all the favourites fell.

# A BROTHER

Being older, I was able for you then,
Won all the contests. You tried hard
And never quite gave in, potential Cain

But less than lethal. Later I was still
Winning, had found in books a new
Arsenal and you, baffled, lost the will

To compete. We grew apart. The eleven plus,
The college years, drove a slow wedge,
Stretching what thin bonds were left between us.

Lately when we meet your talk defines
The ache of dead-ends, of roads not taken.
I note your hands are twice the size of mine.

# SHEEPMAN

Even the barflies move to corner tables,
Mouthing 'Sheepman'. The barman serves,
But grudgingly. Like Mexicans and half-
Breeds I must wear that special hangdog look,
Say nothing.

There is too much cattle country. The range
Is free in theory, cowmen find
Excuses to resent the different.
They claim that cows won't feed where sheep have fed.
Pathetic.

Don't say the outcast has his dignity.
Perhaps it's something not to thrive
On brawn, or trample those whose small stampedes
Hurt no one; such victories are thin, cold
Consolation.

Unbowed I claim my rights—to herd alone,
And be accepted. When I skirt
The rim of cattle drives, salute me,
And when I come to share your bunkhouse fire,
Make room.

# MY FRIEND HAVELOCK ELLIS

My first formal lesson on sex I owe
To my mother. Those faded books she bought
At the auction—sixpence the dozen, tied
With a rough string—hid one volume more
Than she bargained for.
For months I harboured him, forbidden one,
Under the green song sheets from *Ireland's Own*.


He never made the bookshelf, even wrapped
In a brown jacket. Consulted daily
Under clumps of trees beyond the hedge
That foiled the window's eye, his lectures turned
Often on mysteries.
I questioned him again until content
He'd yielded all, tutor and confidant.


Even in those days I knew at heart
How much he bored me. The tadpole-diagrams
He labelled Sperm, and cross-sections of organs
Like the cuts in butchers' windows, were less
Than living.
Still I intoned with a determined bliss
Words like fallopian, ovum, uterus.

The real joy was having such a friend,
Sure to be frowned on were his presence known.
He fed my independence, served a need
The set texts neglected. Nothing left then
But to discard him;
Time for fresh schooling, lessons to begin
In the arms of my new friend, Rosita Quinn.

# AFTER MASS

It's Sunday and the country boys have come
To woo from a distance. Intent, they loiter.
One has re-oiled his bicycle, another
Washed his underpants in the Slane river.

The bridge she sits on is of crumbling stone
And slopes in the water. Swinging her legs
She seems indifferent; intent is all they manage.
Fixed where they are they nudge and scratch and mutter:

'The thatch is on, the tenant should be in.'

# THE SCHOOL HOCKEY TEAM IN AMSTERDAM

The talk of knifed bodies in the canals
Will not shake us, this clean night out of Belfast.
Who will be first, we cry, peering from bridges,
To spot a floating Dutchman? Benign faces
And a different sky sanction such fooling,
Assure us talk's talk and nothing's afloat
But spars and barges.

Someone has broken windows, two street-lamps,
Near our hotel. We note instead the untouched
Bicycles and, next to the pavement, hoardings,
Warehouse walls clear of graffiti.
Brown's card to his mother—windmill, tulips—
Speaks for us all: Brothels and Sex Shops everywhere.
Wish you were here.

# SPOT THE BALL

Once, with a certain pride, we kept attempts
To the minimum. Reason was all:
To trace invisibly the upraised eyes
Of backs and forwards; where the lines converged
To plant our crosses.

Later we combed the stand advertisements
For smudged lettering, or held the thin page
Up to the light to test for shadow.
Those paler patches, blotches near the goal
Could well be erasions.

And, later still, the joking nonchalance,
The stray marks in all the wrong places,
Floodlights and flags and corners that the teams
Had turned their backs on. Even the goalie's crutch
Was not immune.

Four years now and never on the right end
Of a Snowball. Thursday's edition tells
Of prizes bound for places elsewhere.
The 'Belfast man who requests no publicity'
Is always another.

We persevere from habit. When we try
These days our hope's mechanical, we trust
To accident. We are selective
No longer, the full hundred crosses
Filling the sky.

# FANFARES

### 1 *Once a Month*
Suddenly, above the hedge, a head,
Moving at speed. It dips
And rises, further up the lane becomes
A flying bust, and at the next gap
Takes final form:
The District Nurse on a bicycle.


### 2 *Factory Girl*
The bus drums
Between the mouths of lanes.
Finding it slow
A girl springs for the verge,
Trotting already.
Dances are promised.
An hour from now
She'll hear a Morris stop
At the hall door
And must be ready.
Still in her overalls,
With what delight
She spills towards the first shortcut,
Winning another minute for the night.

### 3 Walkers Observed

A winter morning and our talk is stilled
To curious silence. In anoraks
And bright Collegiate scarves three girls
Are passing, the Colonel's daughters
On a Charity Walk.


Mindful of other chores—a path to clear,
Ice to be broken and a pebbled smile
To cheer a snowman—we retreat at last
Into our own daylight. A frozen hedge
Escorts them out of sight.

# IN LIEU OF CAROLS

Setting out in darkness this Christmas Eve
I find the countryside is brewing mist
In all its hollows. Out of it the wet
Lane unravels, hatches every yard
A tree, a fence, the dull outline of fields.
My way is to the shop to buy matches.


Beyond the hedge the black shapes of cattle,
Trampling mudholes, shadow me to the road.
I cannot see their smoky breath, but feel
Its warmth. If there be stars among the sights
The mist has hidden, good! Enough for now
To make my journey following cottage lights.

# STONE

This rough stone the horses scratch against
Did service in a bell-tower on a hill
Before the church toppled.


A farmer picked it from the ruins, deaf
To superstition. In his eye it lodged
Already in a strong building


Below in the yard. Perhaps he rolled it,
Years and years ago, perhaps an ox
Hauled it down to the house


By the spent quarry where it was hewn.
May stones from all ruined churches survive thus,
Whitewashed, in stable walls.

# ILLUMINATION

Scrounging for fallen boughs in the plantation,
I kicked a rotten log out of the rut
Where storms had left it. At once the underside
Became a scare, a crush of jostling things
Tossed to the light, craving the darkness lost.


Stillness returned, and all around the tact
Of filtering sunbeams. Delicate reproach
Breathed in the silence. With the grace it shone
Of skies in a cloud's wake, sunlight in wait
And woods turning slowly into the dawn.

# A DAY IN AUGUST

And still no stronger. Swathed in rugs he lingered
    Near to the windows, gauging distant hills.
Balked by the panes that promised light and flowers,
    The wasps were dying furiously on sills.


A doctor called. She walked him to the doorstep,
    Then sent the children out to gather cones
Under the trees beside the ruined churchyard.
    They romped, unheeding, in the tilted stones.


And now the wheels are turning. They impress
    Tracks that will not outlast the winter's rain.
The siren leaves a wash of emptiness.
    He is lost to the small farms, lane by lane.

# BACKROADS

No one was ever lost on backroads.
Their intrigues end in signposts, farmhouse doors,
The cottages their tributary lanes
Prompt to discover. These bent miles, the closest
Trails they go, are not more subtle
Than the minds that planned, the hands that laid them.


Still at their meetings creeping fields infringe,
An inch more than last year. Briar and branch
Conspire over the tar, the shears' edge,
The scythe's last swing forgotten. Another
Lane meanders to a square the weeds have taken,
Stone ribs in the undergrowth where lives were.

# THE FARM UNDER THE FLOOR

1 *Backroad*
The condemned houses line up for me,
Walking the backroad. At door and sill
Furze spills its surplus, lost for careful hands
To stem invasion.
The snail's tinsel streamer says Just Gone.

Last year the Council tossed the Workhouse,
Built an estate. Tired of making do
Eight families flitted; not sorry
At parting, people left in a hurry.

Still the houses hold their slumped air
Of dereliction. Even sentiment
Has no urge here to rescue better times,
And faced with all their blank evidence
Of loss, I turn away, back to the plain
Sweep of main roads. I won't walk here again.

2 *Smokeless Fuel*
The air of a council estate is charged
With boredom. Where fields were the terraces
Repeat to exhaustion. The eye soon tires
And the heart where corners turn
On the same functional patterns.

Nothing is unexpected, least of all
The week's sad paragraphs of petty crime.
Closer than woods the lorry at the door
With furnacite and anthracite,
A month's smokeless fuel.


3 *Night on the Estate*
Under the lids
Of a Venetian blind
The darkness sees him,
The one man in the terrace
Who is still awake.
Paused in the slats of light
He seems to strain
For tree-sounds and bird-sounds
The street can't offer;
Resumes his beat from table-edge to door,
From door to table.
In the dawn hours, perhaps,
His eyes will close,
These walls accepted.
Till then, his slippered soles
Forgetting stone, the depth of carpet,
He walks again the farm under the floor.

# ORNAMENTS

My mother's council house is occupied
By ornaments. On all flat surfaces
The delft hens roost. Hunched and malignant-eyed
The red dwarfs squat on the mantelpiece,
And panniered donkeys draw their nostrils wide
On mouths that sparkle. The brass bells increase
In cunning mirrors and glass-backed cases.


This the extravagance she must have known
And hoarded in a house where stretching legs
Was luxury, a plaster dog the lone
Flourish that space allowed her. Now she thrives
On detail. For the dog a plaster bone;
The dwarfs have Snow White sweetening their lives,
And today the delft hens have laid delft eggs.

# WINTER OFFERINGS

Mother, it pains me that I must confide
To verse these clarities. We're each alone.
Our speech gutters. More than marriage divides
Us. Each visit home
I measure distances and find them grown.


It's your own fault, really. My good at heart
You grasped the chances that would sunder us.
I'm glad you chose to play the dogged part,
Take on the opposition. Often I wonder
How you prevailed against that blunderbuss


My father. What-was-good-enough-for-him—
The peasant's caution rather than a ploy
To keep me tethered; but you saw how grim
The prospects. Trapped yourself, you rescued me
From lives I guess at. Then, how could I joy


In love so functional, how call it love
That hid and whispered in a tough concern
With Grants and Benefits? So, schooled above
You, I grew up to miss those transferred yearnings.
School's out, but now in retrospect I learn.

Discarded woman, shame is turning me
To wish you mornings, and a folding night
Whose dreams are gentle, sight enough to see
This late guest bowed with winter offerings
Who turns his face into your going light.

# AN UNCLE REMEMBERED

You had no subtlety that I could see;
Thick words, livid with threat, hold
In the memory, your drunken sprees
Those months we roamed the farm, where—old,
Thin, bald—you reared pigs. Bachelor's joy, you sneered,
Regret for the girls you hadn't married.


You came to my wedding, uninvited. Guilty,
I found a seat for you, hoped you'd be civilized.
You ate your fill, cracked your jokes about free
Booze, and made a speech that surprised everyone,
Generous, maudlin. We laughed at your awkward dress,
Your half-hearted passes at a fat waitress,


And laughed too, as the train drew out,
To hear your shout break through, half-sober,
Asking that the first boy be named for you.

# AT THE RECEPTION

Accept my gratitude. I toast the loins
           that wove to make her,
the walls that warmed her growing, held her bloom,
           that humble acre
green to the door, the freshness and the good
its subtle gifts. Accept my gratitude.


Accept my gratitude. I name the days
           that shaped this morning,
the roads that rolled between us, and the hand
           that mapped our turning
into the way our lingering solitude
found company. Accept my gratitude.


Accept my gratitude. I call to mind
           our carefree learning,
those botched and fumbling ardours that were more
           than springtime burning.
I praise the winters, all the tests we've stood
To share this noon. Accept my gratitude.

I toast you, love, and those our ribald guests,
      whose winks are carnal,
whose nudges question shrewdly if my way's
      always so formal.
Be comforted. My plans for your delight
breed in their multitudes. I toast tonight.

# VIRGINS

Supper was quiet. Apart as we'd ever been
We said grace, climbed the stairs
And entered that hour glad of proprieties.


No hurried spendings fathered debts on us
Our wedding night. Our peace passed understanding.
Tensions of two years found their release.


In that quiet room what marked our bed
Implied no loss, no slaughtered innocence—
Only a strain of waiting justified,


All small denials, hoardings of the best.
Love lacked a precedent but found a way,
Surely as first kisses, hair on the chest.

# LOVE ON THE COAST

All night the ocean comes to Kelly's Cove,
A mile from their window. Awake in darkness
Often this first week he hears it moving,
The lingering backwash of a troubled dream,
And turns to hold her. Those graceful depths finding
So rough a mile! Almost he expects to hear them leaving.


Her waking wish: to find his arm flung
Across her pillow, its particular hairs
Dark against linen, sand-stains under the nails.
Her mouth would lap that darkness, leaving there
Its print of love with teeth and wetness.
All night the ocean feeds in Kelly's Cove.

# MRS G. WATTERS

The letters still come for Mrs Watters,
Who must, at one time, have warmed this house
And lived as we do. Mostly small matters—

The rolled calendar that, had she stayed,
Might hang now where I drew the rusted nail,
The catalogues, the last gas bill unpaid—

And always *Mrs* Watters. So for me
The spirit of the house is feminine,
Its whisper of the one who, constantly,

Draws letters that assume she has never gone.
On which I weekly write, without conviction:
'No longer living here. Address unknown.'

# THE MASSAGE PARLOUR

In Personal we read between the blinds
Of the last house in the terrace:
There the Solarium, the Sauna there,
The Herbal Bath, perhaps, under the pane
Whose chalked sign proclaims *Utopia*.


'Wait till we get our hands on you!' the girls
Have pledged. Somewhere between the hall
And back door they are tuning their fingers,
Eve and Natasha from the Lisburn Road
In loose dressing-gowns, a choice of masseuses.


Yet no one seems to enter. When we pass
Business is elsewhere or at other hours.
Once was enough, perhaps, for those who found
Rooms where bulbs brittle even the day,
Where disappointment lives and joys are hollow.


Whatever the cause, transfers are in the air.
This week Natasha's in *Arcadia*,
Welcomed in print by Helga and Marlene.
A gain, they claim, in Friendly Atmosphere.
Eve's at the *El Dorado*, Fully Trained.

# THE POLICE MUSEUM

The stained cutlery and poisoned delft,
Outside their fatal minutes, sit on shelves
And gather mildness. Touring Domestic Murders
We can glean some information,
Read on the printed plaques who stabbed, who crumbled,
The sentence passed. But how are we to know
With pity, fear, their dreadful meaning,
After and before? What's missing is the
Feel of cramped spaces, the ticking of clocks.

# MANTOVANI AT THE MENTAL HOSPITAL

Music on stand-by smoothes the ruffled air
Of broken transmissions. Our minds are drawn
To forget the hands at work on the wires,
The urgent studios seeking to replace
These lush minutes with a contact gone.
We wait, unruffled, not adjusting our sets.


This grey mansion, too, has seemed to hold
A bland composure. Inmates have kept
To courtyards, troubling none with broken faces,
Always invisible beyond the lawn's
Fountain and flowers. Passing we hear music;
Over the bright shrubbery the lilting strings.

# THE EDGE OF WAR

The edge of war in a provincial town
Before I was born: the quarries prospered,
Blasting out the stones to build an airfield.
Camps were constructed, training grounds deployed
In sheltered woodland.

Such headline moments! Eisenhower on tour
And local planes sighting the *Bismarck*;
A Wings-for-Victory Week, mobile canteens.
War was a bracing current in the streams
Of a small county.

And once, in the hours of a sombre dawn,
A crowd at the station. Their faces to
Belfast, haunted by a glow that hung on
The skyline, seemed no more to know the edge
Of local quarrels. In their arms thick

Blankets for the refugees.

# THE AIR-RAID SHELTER

This was the Compound, there are the stone floors
In their last camouflage of bush and briar.
The curved huts have vanished, three decades
Of strangers' drawls gone silent in the drains
Of woodland memory.


Only the air-raid shelter holds its ground
In clearings reoccupied. Scrambling its darkness
It defies the probe of thrusting daylight,
A sunk iron burrow rolling the air,
Perfecting its echo.


To laughing children and the yearly birds
Its ears are vacant. Waiting for sirens
It will never hear the tread of lovers,
The quiet fall of acorns on its head,
Tapping the all-clear.


Its dull mouth reminds us of the need
That shapes such places and is negative.
'Never archaic' seems its cheerless song
Against new foliage. 'The skies are empty
Now, but for how long?'

# THE BARRACKS

The woman tending flowers bends her head,
At work on the lupins. Elsewhere the beds
Are weeded. Turned-up soil darkens the edge
Of lawn and plastered wall. The clipped hedge
At the rear might be suburban.


Once, as we passed, the barracks seemed a cage.
We pitied the sergeant, mourned the sergeant's wife
Her cheerless waiting. How did she bear it,
Sitting out the years in grim detention?
Barren of joy we thought her, till today.


The fences high as the building, awkward bars
Of ramps in the roadway fail now to disturb
Her rapt attention. Yards from the sandbags
And the hidden guns she moves in sunlight,
Her hands in the tall flowers unperturbed.

# WINDOWS

Skylights recline, the shapes of indolence,
The sky they view evasive in its shifts,
As often grey as shining. True, they shed light,


But not to ground-floors, and attic-dwellers are few.
What is it in this rare slate that draws me
From curtained rooms? I find myself today


Tired of bay-windows, climbing the stairs.

# ISLANDS

The week Makarios fell we moved house.
His crisis was not ours or near home.
Caught from the hall those bulletins defined
Less than heaped chairs the time's upheaval.


The Turks invaded. Half-way up a wall
With hammer, nails, my focus of concern
Was hanging pictures. Above the city
Bloomed no paratroops. The streets were empty.


And years from now when people ask how long
We've lived here, we will need no calendars.
A voice, untroubled, in the mind will tell:
We moved in the week Makarios fell.

## MOVING IN

The first act of love in a new house
Is not private. Loving each other
We are half-aware of door and mirror.
Our ecstasy includes the bedside chair,
The air from the landing.


Street-lamp and elm utter leaves on walls
As in no room ever. Theirs is the tongue
Our tongues join in translating. Their message
Is clear: tonight you cannot ignore
The world at the window.


So we love in the knowledge of a city
At a different angle. And sharing
Our bed with furniture and tree we claim
Their perspective, merging our lives here
In their established frame.

# FLOODS

At high tide the sea is under the city,
A natural subversive. The Farset,
Forced underground, observes no curfew,
And, sleepless in their beds, the sullen drains
Move under manholes.


Blame fall on the builders, foolish men.
This strained civility of city, sea, breaks
Yearly, snapped by native rains,
Leaving in low streets the sandbagged doors,
The furnished pavements.

# IN MEMORIAM

**I**
Remembering how your tongue flopped for words
In the wet hollow of a hanging lip
The stroke had left you, directly I would press
To service all soft vowels, richest chords,
And sound the currents of your dumb distress.

My sorrow is, because you lived alone
Locked in that silence, I could never learn
The voice you needed. All I do is trace
The ripples where your speech dipped and was gone,
Remembering the thin lips in your dead face.

**II**
Father, I'm forgetting you. Mind struggles
With the smudge of ten years, that shadow loitering
Off-focus. Squat as a tumulus, you've gone
To ground, the gestures, quirks that spoke of you.
I've no photographs to make you new.

Only this landscape holds you near.
On bank holidays alone I scramble down
The rocks and bare hollows, seeking you.
Your image, half unclouding, clouds again,
And year by year wind wearing stone reminds


Of your going. Loss finds its cadence here.

# PASSING THE CREMATORIUM

Someone is leaving town as clean smoke
This summer morning, too much the drifter
Now to let us know—even if he could—
His destination. Who watched, perhaps, the trail
Of jets in skies another summer
May find already that he's half-way there;
Or thinned instead into a blacker air
The factories muster. Whatever fate
Our leisured thought contrives to fit his journey
Pales with our passing;
Diverts no longer than we take to cruise
Beyond that frail thread, seawards, this summer morning.

# AFTERMATH

Chalk-marks that traced the body's line
Cannot be found, the bricks are plastered bare,
The wind has scoured the alley clean.
What comfort there?


Stains on the doorstep that were red
Grow light as stone, worn by the tread of men.
By foot on foot the ghost is laid.
What comfort then?


Limbs are forgetting limbs they shared
And hearts the hearts that answered them before—
In pulse as if they never cared.
No comfort more.

# UNDER THE STAIRS

Look in the dark alcove under the stairs:
a paintbrush steeped in turpentine, its hairs

softening for use; rat-poison in a jar;
bent spoons for prising lids; a spare fire-bar;

the shaft of a broom; a tyre; assorted nails;
a store of candles for when the light fails.